The dragon king of the sea

The dragon king

of the   sea

Japanese decorative art of the
Meiji period
from the John R. Young collection

Oliver Impey and Malcolm Fairley

Ashmolean Museum Oxford 1991

Exhibition and catalogue sponsored by the
Swire Group and Swire Charitable Trust

JAPAN FESTIVAL
UK
19
91

Oxford, 1 October – 1 December 1991
Ashmolean Museum
Beaumont Street, Oxford OX1 2PH, England

Groningen, 1 February – 12 April 1992
Groninger Museum
Praediniussingel 59, 9711 AG Groningen, The Netherlands

Brussels, 29 April – 28 June 1992
Japanese Pagoda
Avenue van Praet 44, B1020 Brussels, Belgium

New York, 10 October – 22 November 1992
Japan Society Gallery
Japan Society Inc, 333 East 47th Street, New York, NY 10017, USA

British Library Cataloguing in Publication Data

Impey, Oliver R.
        The dragon king of the sea: Japanese decorative art of
        the Meiji period from the John R. Young collection
        I. Title
        745.0952074

        ISBN 1854440071

Designed by Cole design unit, Reading
Set in Frutiger by Meridian Phototypesetting Limited
Printed in Great Britain by Jolly & Barber Limited, Rugby
Bound by Green Street Bindery Ltd, Oxford

Preface

Oxford

This exhibition of a selection of works of decorative art of the Meiji period (1868–1912) from the collection of John R. Young, of Dallas, Texas, is our contribution to the Japan Festival, '91. To some extent, this exhibition breaks new ground, as we believe it to be the first Museum exhibition of such things held in Britain since the great Japan-British Exhibition of 1910, in Shepherd's Bush, London. In particular, we do not know of any exhibition since that date that has had a serious look at Shibayama lacquer.

Our thanks are due first of all to the collector, John R. Young, a pioneer collector in this field. Mr Young was collecting at a time when to like these works was to be considered eccentric, to be lacking in taste. He always selected for reasons of quality. Time has justified his choice, as this selection from his collection shows.

We must thank our generous Sponsor, the Swire Group and Swire Charitable Trust, without whom this exhibition would not have taken place. We are also grateful to Barry Davies Oriental Art for support and assistance in all aspects of the project.

We are grateful to Rosemary Zeeman for writing the chapter on the actual work involved in the making of cloisonné enamel, which we feel will make this specialist craft more accessible to the reader. Lady Zeeman writes as a practicing cloisonné artist herself.

The exhibition will travel to The Groninger Museum, Groningen, in The Netherlands, to The Musées Royaux d'Art et d'Histoire, Brussels, in Belgium and to the Japan Society Gallery in New York, in the United States; to the Directors of those institutions, in particular to Dr Gunhild Avitabile, and to Dr C.J.A. Jörg and Dr Chantal Kozyreff we extend our thanks and hopes that this exhibition will be successful.

We would also like to thank Anne Heseltine and Tsumugi Shoji for the assistance they have given us in their various ways.

Mary Tregear
Keeper, Department of Eastern Art
The Ashmolean Museum, Oxford

Preface

Groningen

The Groninger Museum is well known for its extensive collection of Chinese and Japanese export ceramics. Since some years it has been our policy to give this collection a wide context and to present it as part of a programme of 'East-West Interactions'. In this we focus on the mutual influences in the decorative arts between the Netherlands and Asia between *c.* 1600 and 1900, incorporating, for instance, Japanese export lacquer, Indian chintzes, colonial furniture, Ukiyo-e and examples of chinoiserie and japonisme. Not only do we collect actively in this field, but we have also organised a series of exhibitions to the theme.

Despite the important role of the Netherlands in the distribution of oriental objects and motifs throughout Europe, no other Dutch museum covers this aspect of our cultural past so extensively. Therefore I welcomed the opportunity to participate in the exhibition 'The dragon king of the sea', because it fits so well into our exhibition programme on 'East-West interactions'. The objects shown here represent not only the best quality in each category, but also give an excellent survey of a hitherto rather neglected area of Japanese art that was made for and influenced by the West.

I would like to express my thanks to Mr John R. Young for his generosity in lending part of his splendid collection to this travelling exhibition, thus making it possible for an international public to enjoy these treasures. I would also like to thank the Swire Group and the Swire Charitable Trust who have so greatly helped in realising this project. Thanks are also due to Dr Oliver Impey of the Ashmolean Museum who initiated the exhibition, invited us to participate, co-authored the catalogue and co-ordinated all the work. Lastly I would like to thank our curator Dr Christiaan Jörg, who is responsible for our 'East-West Interactions' programme and who organised everything from this end.

F. Haks
Director, The Groninger Museum

Preface

Brussels

The Royal Museums of Art and History are delighted to present the beautiful exhibition 'The dragon king of the sea; Japanese decorative art of the Meiji period from the John R. Young collection', following the Ashmolean Museum and the Groninger Museum.

This exhibition will be most appropriately shown in the Japanese Pagoda, one of the four outside buildings of the Royal Museums. This Pagoda was built, as was the near-by Chinese Pavilion, by the Parisian architect Alexandre Marcel, on the initiative of King Leopold II. The Pagoda was finished in 1905, the Pavilion in 1909.

Both belong to the same artistic current, namely the fashion for chinoiserie and japonisme inspired by a mirage of the Far East. Although their construction was undertaken by Belgians and the finishing touches added by Parisian decorators, yet the architect sought some degree of authenticity. To this end, some of the interior elements of the Pagoda, such as the carved panels and the finely-worked brass plaques, were made to order in Yokohama.

In 1908, Leopold II presented the Japanese Pagoda and the Chinese Pavilion to the State. Since 1921 they have come under the jurisdiction of the Royal Museums.

The Pagoda, reopened in 1989, receives temporary exhibitions of Japanese art. Thus it seems most appropriate for exhibiting to the public 'The dragon king of the sea'.

We warmly thank Mr John R. Young who has so kindly agreed to the showing of his collection in Brussels and to the Swire Group and the Swire Charitable Trust which has made possible the realisation of this event.

Francis Van Noten
Director, the Royal Museums of Art and History

Preface

New York

The arts of the Meiji period (1868–1912) have been neglected or even despised by admirers and students of Japanese arts for a long time. Art historians very seldom specialise in the field, and exhibitions of the work of this formative epoch of modern Japan have been extremely few.

Meiji art, and especially decorative art, has been considered to be purely imitative or even 'kitsch' and not worthy of collection by serious collectors. This attitude may have caused the careless destruction of many fine pieces. In the last quarter of the past century, during Europe's *belle epoque,* when Japan emerged from the mist and entered the world stage, the attitude was quite different. Westerners travelling in Japan and the numerous visitors to the various World Expositions were thrilled by the sensational artefacts of Japan. Artists and craftsmen of this far-away country competed easily with their European counterparts, each on occasion imitating the other.

It was an extraordinary phenomenon. The Japanese had learned from the West without losing their own traditions and culture. Now, about one hundred years later, we are beginning to appreciate again the art of this fascinating period, without prejudice.

For the possibility of holding this exhibition, I wish to thank most warmly our pioneer collector John R. Young, who for many years has formed his collection by following only his own taste and preferences. He provides us here with the opportunity to admire these jewels of *fin de siècle* taste; metalwork, cloisonné and Shibayama lacquer. I wish also to thank our British sponsors, the Swire Group and the Swire Charitable Trust.

I want to thank Dr Oliver Impey and congratulate him on initiating this exciting project; he and Malcolm Fairley have undertaken the difficult task of preparing the scholarly catalogue. I am grateful to Dr Emily Sano of the Dallas Museum, Texas, who first showed me this marvellous collection.

I am proud of the fact that this will be the first time that an exhibition dedicated to the sophisticated decorative arts of the Meiji period of Japan has been held in New York City.

Dr Gunhild Avitabile
Director, Japan Society Gallery, New York

General introduction

The second half of the nineteenth century was a momentous time for Japan, a time of change towards the assimilation of western influence after two hundred and fifty-odd years of official seclusion. The effect of this hurried 'catching-up' period upon the arts of Japan was no less profound than it was on politics or, say, engineering.

The arts of the preceding Edo period (1600–1868) were produced within a framework of government and of patronage that was based on a system that has been likened to feudalism in Europe. The Tokugawa Shoguns, in effect military dictators, had ruled from their capital in Edo (Tokyo) in the name of the hereditary Emperors whose court was in Kyoto. The great lords, the Daimyo, of the various districts of Japan, especially those who had fought against the Tokugawa in the early seventeenth century, were obliged by the Shogunate to spend half their time in Edo, in a manner similar to that enforced by Louis XIV of France and with similar results. Shogunal policy encouraged conspicuous consumption in order to avoid the accumulation by any one Daimyo of too much power or of too much wealth; this, of course greatly benefited the craftsmen who catered to this demanding clientele. Lower down the social scale, the townsmen, the newly rich businessmen were forbidden the use of expensive or rare materials so that they showed their wealth by the display of the skill of the craftsman rather than by the use of gold.

By the second quarter of the nineteenth century, however, the Shogunate was declining in effective power and it was unable to cope with the supposed threat of western incursion triggered by the arrival of the American Commodore Perry in 1853 with demands for trade agreements and for treaties over the repatriation of shipwrecked seamen. The Treaty of Kanagawa of 1854 was seen by some Daimyo as a betrayal of Japanese sovereignty and the subsequent civil war led to the overthrow of the Shogunate in favour of direct rule by a constitution under the supervision of the Emperor; the Emperor thus gained rule of Japan again after an interval of about eleven hundred years. In fact, of course, rule was by Cabinet, still in the name of the Emperor. The new Government of Japan quickly understood that in order to be treated with consideration by the western nations, rapid modernisation was necessary; in order to achieve this everything possible was reorganised on western lines, western technology was introduced, as was western dress, western painting and western music. Buddhism no longer was the state religion and Buddhist Temples and Buddhist art were, for a time, neglected or even destroyed. It was partly due to a young American, Ernest Fenollosa, who had come to teach philosophy in the newly founded Tokyo University, that this tendency not to value the traditional arts of Japan in this new enthusiasm for all things western, was reversed.

With this reversal came the understanding that western and Japanese art had something to offer to each other; it is the results of this upheaval, followed by a settling down period, and by a process of selection, elimination and creation that we are discussing and exhibiting here. Just as the Post-Impressionist painters took time to come to terms with the new aesthetic and the new conventions of the Japanese woodblock print, going through the phases of indiscriminate copying, selection of motifs for re-use, to the understanding of what the printmaker was trying to do, so the Japanese craftsmen went through phases in the absorption, selection and selective elimination of western influences to the creation of a new Japanese style or series of styles.

Of course the situation was more complex than that; much of what was made by the finest craftsmen of the late nineteenth century in Japan was for foreign buyers, either for a sophisticated tourist trade, a new phenomenon in Japan, or through the medium of the great trade fairs, both domestic and international to which Japan contributed, especially after their success at the World Exposition in Vienna in 1873. According to Baekland (1980), at the Nuremberg Metalwork Exposition of 1885 some 492 works were exhibited by 99 Japanese artists. It was, therefore, much influenced by foreign demand.

Many of the items exhibited here were, presumably, made for such sale. The metalworker Kuroda of Kyoto told Herbert Ponting in 1911 that he sold most of his best pieces to English and French visitors; Namikawa Sosuke seems to have specialised in sales to Americans especially after his conspicuous success at the World's Columbian Exposition in Chicago in 1893. Namikawa Yasuyuki told Ponting that potential sales outstripped production; and these were expensive wares. Hayashi Kodenji brought a group of cloisonné enamels to an exhibition in Glasgow in 1911 and consigned them to a London auctioneer for sale in 1912; number 15 in this catalogue was lot 46 in that sale.

The unprecedented activity of the decorative arts in the late nineteenth century was based, of course, on the solid foundation of the fine craftsmanship of the Edo period. New conditions imposed upon the craftsman by government regulation, for instance the banning of the wearing of swords of 1873, or by loss of patronage through the break-up of the 'feudal system', were met by the new formation of groups of craftsmen to work together such as the Sanseisha company (see no. 11), or into more formal schools (the Tokyo School of Art was opened by the Ministry of Education in 1876). There was also the formation of companies, where either a craftsman would employ other craftsmen (e.g. Namikawa Yasuyuki) or where some enterprising entrepreneur (e.g. Namikawa Sosuke) would employ craftsmen. Even these latter were basically of two types; the Miyao company, for instance (see no. 10) was a manufacturing concern, as was the Inoue company (see no. 6) while others may well simply have commissioned individual works of art from any artist thought appropriate. The Ozeki company (see no. 12), apparently made metalwork and lacquer and possibly even cloisonné.

Interesting confirmation that many of the best metalworkers were craftsmen who had previously been employed in the making of sword furniture is provided by no. 1 here; it was made by four sword-furniture makers adapting themselves to the changed conditions. Hence, perhaps, its air of having been designed by a committee.

Metalwork of the Meiji period was, then, a direct descendent of earlier skills; according to Harada writing in 1911, there were three distinct lines. The first was that of Kyoto, based on the celebrated Goto family and leading to Kano Natsuo (1828–1898); when the Court moved to Tokyo, many of the leading artists also moved thither. The second style was that of Tokyo of the time when the Shogun resided there; the artists were much more prone to adopt new styles than were the conservative Kyoto artists. The third group was the Mito group, whose work, according to Harada is 'characterised by strength and solidity rather than by grace and elegance'. As this exhibition demonstrates, new styles arose within these groups to accommodate the newly introduced western ideas, especially that of realism.

Shibayama lacquer, inlaid with carefully carved materials in relief, was a logical extension of earlier practice, absolutely in tune with the contemporary taste for the conspicuous display of skill in a manner that might have been thought flashy in the Edo period but that was in reality no more gaudy than many products of the Genroku period (1688–1703).

The newcomer was cloisonné. We are firmly convinced of the truth of the story of the 're-invention' of the technique of cloisonné enamel by Kaji Tsunekichi in the 1830s and the subsequent rapid development of the craft from the establishment of its new identity in the mid 1870s to its virtual disappearance as an art form in the decade after 1910. This history is outlined on pages 40–43. This is an extraordinary thing to have happened; it was so rapid and so amazingly technically brilliant. But then, the Meiji was a period of innovation and experimentation. We have been slow to accept some of the products of this period as works of art; it is our hope, and that of the collector of these remarkable works, John R. Young, that this exhibition will accelerate the understanding of these works and that the pieces themselves will give the pleasure to the modern viewer that they undoubtedly gave to the original clients of the artists of the time.

Metalwork

The profound changes brought about by the Restoration of 1868 to both the conditions of work of and to the patronage of Japanese metalworkers was possibly more marked than it was for other craftsmen. The sword-furniture makers had been used to working for an overlord who had usually demanded the best work without much consideration of the costs involved. After all, with the swords thrust, cutting side up, hilt forwards through the sash, the small decorations of the hilt were more than prominent, doubtless revealing to the discerning eye much of the wearer's status. With the proscription of the wearing of swords, all these highly skilled craftsmen were simply out of work. They had to find other outlets for their skill, adapting to the new demands of a public that not only wanted good work, but wanted value for money. No other craftsmen can have been so completely affected by the new conditions save only, perhaps, the carvers of Buddhist images.

That such sword-furniture makers formed themselves into groups is evident from informal groupings such as that of those men who made the *koro* exhibited here as no. 1, probably led by Suzuki Gensuke and by the more formal companies of which one of the finest was the Sanseisha (see no. 11). The Sanseisha was a company that specialised in the highest quality productions, taking two years to make their sole entry in the Second Domestic Industrial Exposition in 1881, 'The dragon king of the sea', the great bronze figure after which this exhibition is named. Brinkley in 1904 has this to say; 'Between 1875 and 1879, some of the finest bronzes – probably the very finest of their kind – ever produced in Japan were turned out by a group of experts working in combination under the firm-name 'Sansei-sha'. Started by two brothers, Oshima Katsujiro (art name Joun) and Oshima Yasutaro (art name Shokaku) in 1875, this association secured the services of a number of skilled chisellers of sword-furniture who had lost their *metier* owing to the abolition of the sword-wearing custom. Nothing could surpass the delicacy of the works executed in the Sansei-sha's *atelier* at Kobinata in the Ushigome quarter of Tokyo. Unfortunately such productions were above the standard of the customers for whom they were intended. Foreign buyers, who alone stood in the market at that time, failed to distinguish the fine and costly bronzes of Joun, Shokaku, and their colleagues from cheap imitations that soon began to compete with them, so that ultimately the Sansei-sha had to be closed'. Brinkley characteristically exaggerates, for the imitations were themselves far from cheap; he must be referring to the works of such factories as the Miyao (see no. 10), where the inlay of the finest work is replaced by fine quality gilding, a much cheaper process. It seems, however, to have been largely true. Brinkley continues 'Foreign demand showed so little discrimination that experts, finding it impossible to obtain adequate remuneration for high-class work, were obliged to abandon the field altogether or to lower their standard to the level of common appreciation, or to have recourse to forgeries'. Brinkley claims that even Joun 'has often been induced to put Seimin's [Murata Seimin 1769–1837] name on objects'.

'The dragon king of the sea' (no. 11) also shows another feature of production methods; credit is given to Takamura Koun, a wood-carver celebrated as one of the finest in Japan (see footnote to no. 11). Koun is known to have made models for bronze casters; it seems likely that his was the model from which Joun worked.

Takamura Koun, as both Harada (1911) and Brinkley (1904) recognised, was important not only for his great skill and for his teaching (he was a Professor at the Tokyo Fine Art School) but for the position he held between the 'pure Japanese' style of former times and the realistic school of the late Meiji. He held the equivalent position in carving that Hashimoto Gaho (1853–1908) held in painting. The Sansei-sha was, indeed, using the finest artists available. Other sculptors than Koun also made works for bronze casters; Brinkley illustrates an ivory figure by Udagawa Kazuo who exhibited bronzes at the St Louis Louisiana Purchase Exposition in 1904 and at the Japan-British exhibition in London in 1910.

The works mentioned above, by Udagawa Kazuo, raise the question of how many of each bronze-casting was produced, a question that we cannot yet answer. The same bronze 'A farmer's wife at lunch' is illustrated in both the St Louis and London catalogues, and also by Harada in 1911. In each of these pictures she is seated on a bronze bench; in the version at the Ashmolean Museum, she sits on a wooden bench, enough faded for it to be likely that it is original and not a replacement. On the London art market recently, there was an ivory figure that may well have been the model, though it was unsigned.

Kazuo belonged to the 'romantic' school of realism, Koun to the 'mid-way' school and Suzuki Gensuke (no. 1) to the more old-fashioned 'pure Japanese' school. The Hattori company and those specialising in inlays of various metal alloys belong to a different branch of the 'pure Japanese' school with far more obvious influences from the traditional sword-furniture makers.

The 'romantic' and 'mid-way' schools are of particular interest for their innovative styles; while both come under the term 'Tokyo School', it is worth attempting to differentiate between them. The 'romantics' usually sculpted images of working people looking happy, prosperous and well-nourished; these may verge on the sentimental, though by no means always. This romantic vision of rural bliss was not closely based upon reality.

The 'mid-way' school of Harada has many similarities with the 'New Sculpture' movement in Europe. Many of the artists had either studied under the teaching of Italian sculptors at the short-lived Kobu Daigaku Bijutsu Gakko (the Engineering College Art School, 1876–1883) or in Europe (e.g. Shinkai Taketaro (1868–1927). Harada illustrates examples in his article on wood and ivory carving (1911); many of these artists also worked in bronze. Into the first group would fall, for example, the idealising work of Yoshida Homei and of Kaneda Kinjiro, while contrasting with these would be the work of Takamura Koun's pupil Yonehara Unkei and of Hiragushi Denchu.

Harada in 1911 did try to draw up three lineages of metalworkers, the Kyoto style, formal, elegant and old-fashioned even in its hey-day; most Kyoto metalworkers moved to Tokyo with the new Government. The Kyoto style was based on the refined work of the Goto school of sword-furniture makers; their most famous representative in the Meiji was Kano Natsuo (1828–1898). Harada's second style was that of Tokyo following the tradition established at the Shogunal court, when a somewhat brash and fashion-conscious style prevailed. The third style was that of Mito; many Mito artists went to Tokyo and exerted a great influence. Harada lists Shomin and Bisei (Unno Yoshimori) as two of the finest Tokyo artists who learned from Mito teachers; he makes no attempt to classify further. Clearly there were no hard and fast distinctions to be drawn save between individual artists.

And if Joun was signing Seimin (and their work was, according to Brinkley, equally good) on occasion, how are we to set up criteria of attribution today? It may well be that Brinkley misinterpreted this copying as forgery; may it not have been emulation and homage, a well-established custom in China and Japan?

Brinkley's point about the impossibility of selling the finest quality metalwork is important; Meiji metalwork seems to 'peak' in quality earlier than do either cloisonné or Shibayama. Was it simply too costly to make, was the effort put into the finest work visible to so few people that no one would buy it?

We must regard the work of, say, the Miyao company as of the second rank; quality of detail has been sacrificed for reasons of simple economics. But it should be added that the work of such 'second rank' companies was still of extremely high quality. If the style is to be criticised as too obvious, too popular, that is another matter; there were different levels of taste and of price. This is phenomenon that we have noted elsewhere.

We do not have much information on how much these things actually cost. Ponting, visiting Kuroda in Kyoto, was shown a plaque inlaid with a scene of the Bay of Enoura; price £8. When he praised it as better than anything he had seen in any other shop. Kuroda commented 'Do you know what I think of it? What you are looking at is rubbish. No Japanese collector would bestow a second glance on it. Now I will show you what a Japanese, *who knows,* would call good work'. He showed Ponting another, costing £30; the 'difference was not apparent at the first glance, and only by careful scrutiny could I see the immense amount of skill lavished upon the one, which the other lacked . . . Though the thicker gold and silver used, and the better quality of the bronze, increased the value, yet the extra cost was mainly due to the workmanship expended on it'.

Kuroda commented that most of his work was bought by English and French visitors; vases and plaques were the favourite pieces. He offered *shibuichi* cigarette- or card-cases 'inlaid with some such simple design as a peasant carrying a load of firewood, or a pair of fighting-cocks; but one must pay at least £15 to £20 for it if one wants the finest work'.

An account of the purchases made by a Dutch naval officer who was in Japan in 1897, S.van Lennep, lists several pieces of metalwork. Van Lennep was, perhaps, buying third quality things; he bought, in Yokohama, two bronze eagles for $6.00, two bronze partridges for $5.00, one bronze pheasant for $7.00 and another bronze eagle for $5.00. These were clearly at the lower end of the market. The best was too expensive for van Lennep, if he even saw it; Brinkley makes it clear that the best was too expensive for anyone.

1
Koro and cover
Signed Tokyo Hokisai Suzuki Gensuke
saku; also Harushima Nobumasa with
kakihan, Harada Masatoshi with
kakihan, Ritsumin with *kakihan* and
Shuraku with seal Shiun
Height 82.5 cm
Dated Meiji 10 (1877)

A large inlaid *shakudo* and gold *koro* and cover, by Suzuki
Gensuke, the body of square section decorated with foliate
diaper-work inlaid with two panels depicting the butterfly
bugaku dance and a festival drum, raised on a multi-tiered
pedestal applied at mid-section with gold dragons above a
plinth with corner brackets cast with gilt shishi amongst
rocks and waves above twelve small reserves of the animals
of the Zodiac, in turn above a wide band of rolling waves
with gilt foam, the base with four long reserves of dragons
and a signature medallion. The censer applied with large
handles in the form of flowering Paulownia branches, the
cover cast in the form of rocks decorated with gold lichen
and surmounted by a large gilt phoenix.

The original concept of this elaborate koro was probably that of
the artist whose signature appears on the base, Suzuki Gensuke.
This must be Suzuki Gensuke 1st (?1834–1914) who used the *go*
(art name) Hokisai. He lived in Ikenohata in Tokyo and was
succeeded in 1887 by his son who also (confusingly) used the
same *go.* He exhibited a large pair of *shakudo* flower vases at the
first Domestic Exhibition in 1881. Brinkley (1904) praises
Gensuke as an inventor of new techniques.
Harushima Nobumasa (dates unknown) had been a maker of
kozuka knife handles and of *menuki* fittings. He was a pupil of
Miyata Nobukiyo who had in turn been a pupil of Goto
Mitsuyasu.
Harada Masatoshi appears to be unrecorded.

Serizawa Ritsumin (d. after 1887) was a pupil of Tenmin, and had
made *menuki* and *fuchi-kashira.*
Ozawa Shuraku (1830–1894) was also a pupil of Tenmin and had
made *tsuba, fuchi-kashira* and *kozuka.*
It is interesting to have confirmation of the transition in early
Meiji times of metalworkers who specialised in the fittings of the
sword becoming makers of elaborate and often large objects of
very fine quality for a new market. With the banning of the
wearing of swords, and before the revival of the fashion for small
fittings by the western market, many such artists had to turn
their skills to this new field. This *koro* bears decoration in many of
the techniques typical of the sword-furniture makers' repertoire,
used with no diminution of skill. Contrast this with the slightly
later works by the large companies set up to exploit this market
at a lower level, notably the Miyao company (see no. 10) where
the work gives the appearance of this very high quality, but by
the use of less sophisticated techniques.
This magnificent *koro* must have been made for an exhibition,
possibly that of the International Exposition in Paris of 1878 or
of the First Domestic Exposition of the same year.

2
Plaque
Unsigned
Diameter 32.7 cm
Circa 1870

An inlaid copper plaque in high relief with a scene of Handaka Sonja appearing on the back of a dragon to his brother Chuda Handaka Sonja and an *oni* attendant standing on a rocky promontory, worked in *shakudo*, *shibuichi*, silver, copper and gilt.

It is unusual to find a piece of such quality unsigned. It would be reasonable to attribute this to one of the companies who commissioned high quality works from the best artists, possibly to Unno Moritoshi (1834–1896) originally of the Mito school, who occasionally executed commissions for the Ozeki company.

3
Bottle vases
Sealed Jomi
Height 18.4 cm
Circa 1885

A pair of bronze bottle vases by Jomi Eisuke decorated with numerous butterflies, moths and dragonflies in *shakudo, shibuichi, sentoku,* silver and copper, the details in gilt and *iroe-honzogan* (flat inlay in many metals), on a ground with silver and *shakudo kirigane* (metal foil cut into square or rectangualr shapes).

Jomi Eisuke worked in Kyoto. He exhibited twelve pieces in the Second Domestic Industrial Exposition in 1881. Ponting, writing before 1911, states that 'At Jomi's one can see inlaid work no less perfect than Kuroda's; and Jomi is also the king of workers in beaten copper.

Jomi gave me one day as instructive a lesson in beaten-copper work as Kuroda gave me in bronze. He showed me two quite plain but very tastefully designed vases, globular shaped, with long thin necks. The bodies were about four inches in diameter, and the necks perhaps six inches long and half an inch thick. They were to all intents and purposes a pair, exactly alike, yet one was five times the price of the other. The reason was that, though both were beaten out of a flat sheet of copper, one of them had the base brazed on, whilst the other was made in one piece. One need not be an expert to realise that a copper vase, with a large round body, a base, and a long and very thin neck, beaten out of one single sheet of metal, must be the acme of skill of the metal-beater's craft, and therefore worth much more than an apparently similar article in which the greatest difficulty was avoided by having a large open base through which to work.'

For a similar differential between the best and the second best, in cloisonné enamel, see the footnote to no. 21, where Shibata has used the easier technique, whereas his former employer Namikawa Yasuyuki did not do so.

Harada (1910) illustrates a pair of vases with comparable decoration by Toyokawa Mitsunaga (1850–1923), placing him in the Tokyo group of metalworkers of this period.

4
Kodansu
Signed Kyoto Inoue with maker's seal
Height 18.4 cm
Circa 1880

An inlaid bronze *kodansu* decorated with *manji* diaper-work in gold *honzogan* inlaid with panels on the sides and on the door with birds, flowers and animals in *iroe-takazogan*. The interior with three wood-lined drawers inlaid with metal plaques.

This is a conventional shape utilised by the Inoue company to demonstrate the skill of the metalworkers who must have been sword-furniture makers.

5
Kodansu
Signed Dai Nihon Kyoto shi Otsuno sei
Height 16 cm
Circa 1880

An inlaid iron *kodansu* with two open-panelled doors enclosing seven small gilt-lined drawers with silver chrysanthemum pulls decorated with shaped panels of Zodiac animals and with panels of birds reserved on a floral ground, worked in two tones of of gold and silver *honzogan* and with a gilt overhead handle.

The Otsuno company worked in the manner of the better-known Komai company, making work of a high standard of quality.

6
Hanging vase
Signed on a silver tablet Inoue sei
Height 24.8 cm, excluding chain
Circa 1885

An inlaid bronze hanging vase of bell shape, with a broad collar of *rui* lambrequins and with hooks below the base, suspended by a linked silvered metal chain, the body decorated in relief with a dragon in clouds, partially worked in silver and with gilt details.

The shape may be that of an incense-burner or of a hanging flower-vase.
The Inoue company was somewhat similar to the Miyao company (see no. 10), making good pieces of second quality for a westernizing market. (See also no. 4).

7
Charger
Signed on the reverse Dai Nihon
Kyoto shi, Tomeie Shikobe saku
Diameter 76 cm
Circa 1885

A large bronze charger decorated in relief with a procession of warriors accompanying a *kago* carriage worked in silver, copper, *shakudo, sentoku* and gilt.

The name of the artist appears to be unrecorded.

8
Koro and cover
Sealed Hattori
Height 20.3 cm
Circa 1900

A bronze tripod *koro* and pierced cover, decorated with a scene of the Itsukushima Shrine in *takazogan* worked in *shakudo*, *shibuichi*, gilt-bronze and copper on a faint *mokume* (wood-grain) ground. The lid reticulated with flowers in similar soft metals.

The Hattori company who made this *koro* should not be confused with the name of the cloisonne-maker Hattori Tadasaburo.

9
Koro and cover
Signed on a gilt plaque Yoshizuka
Height 14.7 cm
Circa 1890

An enamelled silver and iron *koro* and cover, the lobed body inset with three reticulated silver filigree panels brightly enamelled with stylised flowers and phoenix and with gold wire, the cover similarly decorated and surmounted by a figure of Jurojin.

10
Yoshitsune
Signed in a cartouche Dai Nihon Tokyo
Miyao sei, Katsutoshi saku
Height 126 cm
Circa 1895

A large standing figure of Yoshitsune holding a spear, his left hand to his *katana*, the face and hands richly patinated in pale brown, the eyes of *shakudo* and with gilt details. Standing upon a wooden base with gold lacquer scrollwork.

The Miyao company, formed by Miyao Eisuke was perhaps the largest and most successful of the companies that specialised in quality pieces of the second rank; that is, well cast and carved pieces that were decorated not in sword-furniture makers' techniques of inlay, but with gilt details instead. The Miyao company exhibited at many trade fairs, including the Second Domestic Industrial Exposition in Tokyo in 1881.
The names of the various workmasters of the Miyao company are rarely recorded. Katsutoshi may be either Nakajima Katsutoshi or Mizuno Katsutoshi, both of whom are recorded as working in Tokyo at this time.
About Minamoto no Yoshitsune, one of the most famous warriors of Japan, a whole series of legends have grown; he was a favourite subject for heroic depictions such as this.

11
The dragon king of the sea
Signed by the Sanseisha company of
Tokyo
Height 135 cm, width 101.5 cm
Dated 1879–1881

A massive bronze group by Oshima Joun and others of the Emissary of Ryujin, the dragon king of the sea, attended by a fabulous sea-creature of almost human form, presenting the Jewel of the Tides to Takenouchi no Sukune, the Minister to the Empress Jingo. The Emissary holds out the jewel on a circular stand; he wears an elaborate helmet surmounted by a dragon and a long flowing cloak made with sea-creature motifs. The attendant with a spiny, fish-like mask holds a tall palm fan, his costume a girdle of lobster suspending a sea-weed skirt. The warrior nobleman holds a bow and arrows and is dressed in half-armour. All three stand on a base of rocks on which rest crabs, snails and terrapins, set on a rectangular plinth with corner brackets in the form of dragons in turn resting on an inswept base supported by four fantastic winged sea-dragon feet. The underside with two inscriptions in square cartouches and a low-relief scene of fishes and a prawn in waves.

The inscriptions read 'Made by the Sansei-sha of Tokyo and exhibited at the Second Domestic Industrial Exposition', and 'Started at the beginning of the 9th month (September) of Meiji 12 (1879) and finished in the first month (January) of Meiji 14 (1881). Artist Oshima Joun assisted by Takamura Koun and Hasegawa Siu'un'.
According to Brinkley (1904), the Sanseisha company was started between 1875 and 1879 by Oshima Katsujiro (1858–1940) whose art name (go) was Joun and his brother Oshima Yasutaro (art name Shokoku) at Kobinata in the Ushigome district of Tokyo.
At the Second Domestic Industrial Exposition, held in Ueno Park, Tokyo, from 1 March to 30 June 1881, the list of exhibitors records that the Sanseisha company of Takekawa-cho, Kyobashi, Tokyo exhibited only an 'Okimono of Ryujin, lost wax process, by Oshima Katsusaburo'. The artist Oshima Joun also used the name Katsujiro, but not the name Katsusaburo, a name which is listed

in the same record as in the Morimura Ichitaro company. As the Sanseisha only exhibited the one piece it is beyond doubt that the okimono of Ryujin referred to is the piece described and exhibited here, and the error in the name of the artist is due to mistranscription.
Oshima Joun had been a pupil of his father Oshima Takajuro, becoming one of the great figures of late Meiji, Taisho and early Showa sculpture. He was a teacher at the Tokyo Art School, becoming Professor in 1919, and a member of innumerable committees and panels of judges at exhibitions and competitions. Takamura Koun (1852-1934) took premier place, according to Harada (1910) among the individual artist-carvers [in wood and ivory] of his day. 'He stands midway between the extreme realistic school of modern movements and the idealistic school of former times . . . He was originally a Busshi, that is, one who carves Buddhistic images . . . His work is characterised by bold chisel strokes expressive of force and strength . . . Among his numerous works, that which may be regarded as his masterpiece is a large monkey, ten feet high, now in Nara Museum . . . Koun is now [1910] a court artist, and appears to have retired from the active arena, devoting his time to teaching at the Tokyo Fine Art School, being a head professor there.' Brinkley points out that Koun carved subjects for metalworkers; it would be interesting to know just what part Koun played in this joint-work.
Hasegawa Siu'un (dates unknown) is recorded as a pupil of Oshima Joun.
A somewhat similar massive bronze, apparently representing the same subject, is inscribed with a lengthy account of its iconography, there described as the receipt by Susano-o no Mikoto of the Yasakani no magatama in the form of a crystal ball from Kobaaki no Mikoto and an attendant. This bronze is signed by another artist (Otake Norikuni), but its similarity to the bronze shown here is evident. (Fairley, 1991, no. 30.)

12
Vase
Sealed Ozeki sei, signed Jitsumei saku
Height 30.5 cm ·
Circa 1895

An inlaid *shakudo* and translucent cloisonné enamel vase by Jitsumei for the Ozeki company, the *shakudo* body with two gold dragons among clouds and inset with two translucent enamel panels with ducks in relief worked in gold wire flying above or swimming among fishes and waterplants, the neck and foot enamelled with formal floral motifs.

The Ozeki company was an entrepreneurial one, that commissioned work from various artists, usually of the finest quality. No cloisonné company, not even large concerns such as the Ando company could alone have made such a composite piece as this.
Ozeki Yahei had been a pipemaker; no information is available on Jitsumei, though presumably he was a metalworker. The lines of the water and the scales of the fish are engraved in order to show through the translucent enamel (see p. 42)

13
Phoenix
Signed on a gilt tablet Kantei
Height 21 cm
Circa 1900

A silver model of a phoenix standing upon one leg on a rock washed by waves, with gold, *shakudo* and gilt details.

Okimono in silver are uncommon.

14
Vases
Signed Sato Kazuhide kinkoku
Height 24.8 cm
Circa 1900

A pair of inlaid silver Imperial Presentation vases by Sato Kazuhide of high shouldered form, carved and applied with flowering paulownia and with chrysanthemums in tones of gold and in *shakudo*. The necks with applied gold chrysanthemum mon.

This form of vase, with the slightly concave shoulder, is found in other materials also bearing the Imperial mon; see, for instance the pair of cloisonné vases by Namikawa Sosuke in the British Museum. It is tempting to suggest that this was a shape favoured by the Imperial Household; examples of the shape that do not bear the Imperial mon have not been found.
Sato Kazuhide (1855–1925) was a pupil first of Iwamoto Ikkan and then of Ozaki Kazuyoshi; he is said to have specialised in miniature pieces and to have made many objects for the Imperial Household. The suffix *kinkoku* signifies the respect of the carver, or the honour he felt in carrying out this commission.

Cloisonné

The process of the making of cloisonné enamel is described by Rosemary Zeeman, a British cloisonné artist, in the Appendix on pages 104–109. The craft of cloisonné enamel is not an old Japanese skill; the Hirata family of sword-furniture makers had used small-scale cloisonné decoration on *tsuba* and other small fittings as early as the seventeenth century, but not, apparently, on larger items. No other cloisonné makers of anything of any scale are recorded until the 1830s and yet it has not been universally accepted that this was a new departure for the Japanese. James Bowes, in two books, 'Japanese enamels' in 1884, and 'Notes on *shippo*' in 1895 obfuscated the matter by claiming that the Japanese had made cloisonné vessels earlier than the early nineteenth century, in contradiction to all other opinion in Japan of the time, and this claim is sometimes repeated today. There is no documentary evidence in favour of Bowes' opinion, nor any securely dated specimen.

In the 1830s, Kaji Tsunekichi (1803–1883) of Owari (present day Aichi-ken), near Nagoya, began to experiment with imported Chinese and (supposedly) Dutch enamels in order to be able to make imitations. Under his most important pupil, Hayashi Shogoro, the village of Toshima, near Nagoya, became such a centre for the craft that it was popularly re-named *Shippo-mura*, Cloisonné village. Nagoya remained the main centre for the craft, developing under two of Shogoro's pupils, Hayashi Kodenji (1831–1915) (for an example of his work, see no. 16) who started his own factory and Tsukemoto Kaisuke (1828–1898) who taught Namikawa Yasuyuki (1845–1927) and was later employed by Namikawa Sosuke (1847–1910), both of whom we shall discuss below.

Tsukemoto moved to Tokyo to work in the German-owned Arens company, but moved back to Nagoya when that company went out of business following the loss of its chief chemist Gottfried von Wagener (1831–1892) in 1879, when he worked for the Nagoya cloisonné company, the Shippo Kaisha. Some enamellers set up factories in Yokohama (see no. 16 for a work by Kawano Yoshitaro of Yokohama), others moved to Tokyo (Namikawa Sosuke, nos 23 and 24) or to Kyoto (Namikawa Yasuyuki, nos. 18, 19 and 20). Nagoya retained the companies of Ota Tamashiro, Hayashi Kodenji (no. 16) and of Ando Jubei (no. 26).

All cloisonné makers in Japan thus ultimately depended on the teaching of Kaji Tsunekichi in Nagoya. Kaji and his immediate followers made cloisonné in dark muddy colours in dense overall patterns, using the cloisons simply as divisions of one colour from another. The effect was fussy. In the mid 1870s more use was made of paler colours, perhaps closer to the Chinese colours, and there was more of a pictorial element set against a single colour background. Compare the works of Hayashi Kodenji dated 1871 and 1875 illustrated by Coben and Ferster (1982) as plates 47 and 51. Also compare the two cups enamelled on porcelain for the World Fair in Vienna of 1873 with the pair of vases from the World Fair in Paris of 1878, all in the Österreichisches Museum für angewandte Kunst, Vienna, illustrated by Avitabile (1981) as plates 158 and 161, where the latter has a white ground. Even in this pair of vases, the colours are poor and the background is mottled. But the progress is clear. In 1883 at the Amsterdam World Fair, Namikawa Sosuke won a gold medal for a pair of vases with flowers on a pale blue ground (not in wireless cloisonné, see footnote to no. 22) which are illustrated by Fairley (1990), as plate 38. The background was becoming more important; by 1911 Ponting pointed out that Namikawa Yasuyuki was so famous for his even-coloured dark backgrounds that the pictorial elements were greatly reduced (see footnote to no. 19). Apparently the black and the dark red grounds were the most difficult to make.

It is this rapid development of the skill of the craft over the last quarter of the nineteenth century and the first ten or fifteen years of this century that is so remarkable.

Namikawa Yasuyuki of Kyoto was the man who brought the plain even-coloured background to perfection. The even background allowed the picture to be set against a plain, contrasting colour without distracting (because meaningless) cloisons. At first, in the late '70s and early '80s, these colours had been mottled, and this effect, because unavoidable, was sometimes exaggerated and emphasised. See, for instance, the *koro* by Ando Jubei illustrated by Harada (1911) as the colour plate opposite page 272 and by Coben and Ferster (1982) as plate 158. By the mid '80s, this problem, in turn, had been solved, and the colours could be clear and bright or richly dark (see no. 19).

In the early 1880s, Namikawa Sosuke (no relation to Namikawa Yasuyuki) took control of the Shippo Kaisha of Nagoya and moved to a new factory in Tokyo. In doing so, he had acquired as artists Tsukemoto Kaisuke and his sons Jinsuke and Jinkoro; this family is credited with the invention of a method of concealing or dispensing with wires so that a gradation of one colour into another was achievable, eventually even over large areas. This wireless cloisonné, called *musen,* was first exhibited, by Sosuke, in 1889. At the Third National Domestic Exposition in 1890, Sosuke's *musen* plaques imitating the works of several famous Japanese painters caused a sensation. See no. 22, of slightly later date.

Namikawa Yasuyuki was not one of the many imitators of *musen.* He preferred to make the wire part of the design, an integral part of the overall pattern, by the careful use of gold or

Namikawa Yasuyuki in his workshop (far right)
photographed by Ponting (1911)

silver wire that was not only shaped but tapered where necessary. Yasuyuki was an artist who himself worked closely with every object, as Ponting (1911) bears evidence (see footnote to no. 20). Sosuke, by contrast was an entrepreneur, an employer of others, and there is no evidence that he was himself engaged in the artistic activities of his factory; clearly he must have retained artistic control of the output, as a 'house style' is very evident.

Another new invention was that of low relief, *moriage;* this has been credited both to the Hattori factory and to the Ando factory, supposedly by Kawade Shibataro (see nos. 25 and 26). Certainly pieces decorated with *moriage* were shown by Ando Jubei at the St Louis Louisiana Purchase Exposition of 1904.

If surface decoration had by now been exploited to the full, the invention of first translucent and then transparent enamels enabled the decoration to be carried back to the body. The surface of the silver, copper or even gold body could be decorated with engraving (see no. 12) or in *repousse* (see no. 28). The use of transparent enamel, called *tsuiki-jippo* produced some very startling effects, somewhat changing the character of cloisonné.

The final chapter in this progression — this progression of skill but not always, perhaps, of good taste — was reached with the adoption of the techniques of *plique à jour* enamel, *shotai-jippo,* where the whole metal body is removed after firing, an extraordinarily risky process, to leave the enamel and the wires only, fully translucent. Ando Jubei saw this technique used at the World Fair in Paris of 1900; he bought a piece by Fernand Thesmar from which Kawade Shibataro is said to have been able to imitate the procedure.

Cloisonné of good quality was difficult to produce; Sosuke emphasised these difficulties to the reporter of the New York Herald in 1898 (see footnote to no. 23), citing the high wastage rate as an explanation of supposedly high prices. Namikawa Yasuyuki showed Ponting in 1911 'a pair of vases decorated with an old time feudal procession, an order from the Emperor which had taken his foremost artist over a year to complete'. Hayashi wrote in 1912 that the *koro* exhibited here as number 16 had taken almost six months to make and had required over 51 shades of enamel pastes. Good cloisonné had to be expensive. Ponting was shown by Yasuyuki some pieces that 'ranged in price from five to fifty pounds, a large piece of the latter value being about fifteen inches [(38 cm)] high, and decorated, on a deep blue ground, with a design of white and purple drooping wistarias . . . The larger pieces were in no way inferior to the smaller ones . . .'

Ironically, but not unusually, it was the very success of cloisonné that brought about its demise as an art form; the acclaim accorded to Japanese cloisonné at the various world fairs led to the demand for cheap imitations. Factories sprang up for the mass-production of poor quality items. By 1915 only the Ando company was making any cloisonné of any quality. The hey-day of this unique art had been some thirty-five years at the most.

15
Koro and cover
Unsigned
Height 46.5 cm
Circa 1900

A large cloisonné enamel *koro* and cover, hexagonal, with a short everted neck and tapering body raised on a high bracketted foot and with large side handles. The body decorated with pheasants under a flowering cherry intertwined with wistaria, the reverse with pigeons and sparrows in a maple tree, worked in gold and silver wire and in many colours on a dark blue ground. The pierced lid similarly worked with butterflies on a ground of scrolls and flowers, the handles with scroll-work and the elaborately shaped foot with bands of flowers and geometric patterns above large butterfly motifs.

Following the 'rediscovery' of the processes of the making of cloisonné enamel by Kaji Tsunekichi (1803–1883), the village of Toshima near Nagoya specialised in its manufacture to such an extent that it was often called Shippo-mura (Enamel village). Nagoya remained a cloisonné centre, and three of the major factories were located there; that of Ota Tamashiro, that of Hayashi Kodenji and that of Ando Jubei. This westernishing *koro* might be attributed to any of these factories, but the *koro* illustrated by Hayashi (1911) opposite page 272 is similar enough to the present *koro* for us to follow an attribution to Ando Jubei.

16
Jar and cover
Signed Nagoya Hayashi tsukuru
Height 16 cm
Circa 1905–1910 ·

A cloisonné enamel jar and cover by Hayashi Kodenji (1831–1915) decorated with birds in and flying around flowering trees and with elaborate borders, worked in gold and silver wire on a midnight-blue ground, and applied with silver mounts.

This piece was included in an exhibition in Glasgow in 1911. As the Glasgow Exhibition of that year was almost exclusively composed of materials relating to the glories of the British Empire, we are unable to suggest exactly where this exhibition was held. The whole 'large and valuable collection of Japanese Cloisonné Enamel from the Glasgow exhibition' was 'Offered for Sale by Mr. K. Hayashi of Nagoya' through Messrs Glendining & Co., Limited on Friday, the 19th of April, 1912.

The jar here was lot 46; 'Cloisonné jar with minute decoration of maple tree, cherry blossoms, chrysanthemums and sparrows, outlined with solid gold and silver. There are over 51 different shades of enamel pastes used on dark blue ground; it required almost six months' labour to accomplish the work; 6 ins. high, by K. Hayashi. *(See illustration)*'

17
Vases
Signed Kawano tsukuru
Height 24.8 cm
Circa 1890

A pair of cloisonné enamel vases by Kawano Yoshitaro, each of tall shape and of rounded hexagonal section, profusely decorated with a large number of duck on a stream surrounded by and under numerous flowers and flowering trees, worked in silver wire on a black ground, applied with silver mounts.

Kawano Yoshitaro worked in Yokohama, more accessible to foreign tourists than was Nagoya, and the extreme elaboration of the scene, with its profusion of small detail that does not contribute to the overall shape contrasts strongly with the more austere taste of Kyoto.
Kawano used a special motif of small dots of silver to add sparkle to the piece, by the use of short rods of silver wire fused to the body in the same way as were the cloisons.

18
Kodansu
Unsigned
Height 10.8 cm, width 11.5 cm
Circa 1893

A cloisonné enamel *kodansu* attributed to Namikawa Yasuyuki, with an arched body and single door, decorated on the exterior with formal chrysanthemums and paulownia flowers on a black ground, the interior of the door and the fronts of the three drawers with birds, flowers and maple on a blue ground, all worked in silver wire.

The attribution to Namikawa Yasuyuki (1845–1927) rests partly on the vase dated 1893 in the Tokyo National Museum which bears similar decoration and is also attributed to Yasuyuki (see Coben and Ferster pl. 96). Similar designs are illustrated in his design book *Kyo shippo monyo shu*, pages 96 and 98.

19
Vase
Signed Kyoto Namikawa
Height 22.8 cm
Circa 1905–1910

A cloisonné enamel vase by Namikawa Yasuyuki of slender baluster form and with a narrow neck, decorated with a branch of flowering cherry on which sits a single bird, on a black ground and worked in tapering gold wire, applied with *shakudo* mounts.

The work of Namikawa Yasuyuki of this period represents the high point of so-called standard cloisonne, both in the skill of application, particularly of the plain-coloured grounds and in the sparse decoration in quiet good taste, so different from much contemporary work. Yasuyuki also perfected the use of shaped gold wire, tapering the ends of the wires according to position, so that the wires become an essential part of the design, not merely an outline.

Ponting writing in 1911 of Namikawa's workshop, might almost have been describing this piece; '. . . the wiring of a design had just been finished – the silver vase which formed the base being beautifully filigreed in relief with gold ribbon. Namikawa's fame rests as much on the lustre and purity of his monochrome backgrounds as on the decoration of his ware; therefore this gold enrichment covered but a portion of the surface. It was simply a spray or two of cherry-blossoms, among which some tiny birds were playing. That was all; yet even in this state, as it stood ready for the insertion of the enamels, it was a thing of beauty, for every feather in the diminutive wings and breasts was worked, and every petal, calyx, stamen, and pistil of every blossom was carefully outlined in gold, forming, for the reception of the coloured paste, a network of minute cells, or *cloisons,* from which the art derives its name'.

20
Jar and cover
Signed Kyoto Namikawa and with the
engraved date 1911
Height 8.4 cm
Dated 1911

A cloisonné enamel jar and cover by Namikawa Yasuyuki decorated with pigeons among pinks worked in gold wire on a black background and applied with silver mounts.

This piece, with its date, is of key importance in the dating of this style.

Yasuyuki's production can never have been large; Ponting, in 1911, wrote 'Namikawa's output is so small that the demand for it from visiting connoisseurs and collectors is sometimes more than equal to the supply. There is no catering for the trade'. Ponting also described Namikawa's workshop in Kyoto 'a spotless room, twenty feet in length, the floor covered with padded mats, on which, bending over tiny tables, were ten artists . . . Close by them were two figures, rubbing and polishing.

This was Namikawa's entire staff.

In this room could be seen the whole process by which enamelled ware, called 'cloisonné', was produced, except the firing.'

Ponting's photograph shows one end of the room 'shelved for the reception of the bronze [sic] and silver vases that are used as foundation for the enamel-work, and for some hundreds of bottles filled with mineral powders of every shade and colour. These were the materials for the enamels'.

In the firing-room, Ponting saw 'two small furnaces, and in the centre of the room a brick platform on which a kiln could be rapidly made, from firebricks, for any sized muffle that might be desired'.

'Although Namikawa now does little work himself except the designing and firing,' wrote Ponting 'he closely supervises each piece during its entire execution'. A design book surviving from Yasuyuki's shop, the *Kyo shippo monyo shu,* suggests that this may not always have been the case, and that some designs at least were by others, notably Nakahara Tessen.

21
Vase
Unsigned, but attributed to Shibata
Height 21 cm
Circa 1890–95

A cloisonné enamel vase with tapering ovoid body and everted neck decorated with formal trailing purple and white wistaria flower-sprays and leaves above small flowering plants, the neck with bands of formalised flowers and butterflies, worked in silver wire on a black ground and applied with shakudo mounts.

The slightly simplified method of construction, whereby the base is applied under the foot, rather than the base being an integral part of the construction suggests the attribution to Shibata, who had worked in Yasuyuki's workshop, rather than to Yasuyuki himself. The style represents a stage between that of the kodansu (no. 18) attributed to Yasuyuki and the developed style of the 1910s (nos. 19 and 20).

22
Tray
Sealed Namikawa Sosuke
Width 30 cm
Circa 1895–1900

A cloisonné enamel tray, of kidney shape, by Namikawa Sosuke decorated with a black and a white pigeon worked in gold and silver wire and in wireless *(musen)* technique on a graduated orange to grey ground; the painting after Watanabe Seitei. The reverse with dark brown matt enamel with roundels of formal motifs in colours.

Namikawa Sosuke (1847–1910) did not invent the *musen* (wireless) technique of enamelling, rather he was able to use the work of others as an entrepreneur. The technique seems to have been invented by Tsukemoto Kaisuke (1828–1898) and his sons Jinsuke and Jinkuro who worked for the Nagoya Cloisonné company; when Sosuke took over this company in 1887 he was able to employ the Tsukemotos, moving the factory to Tokyo.

Thus the diploma he won at the Second Domestic Exhibition in 1881 cannot have been for *musen*. His entry then was probably closely similar to the vases for which he won a gold medal in 1883 at Amsterdam (See Fairley, 1990, no. 38). He first exhibited *musen* in 1889 at the Bijutsu Kyokaiten (Association of Fine Arts Exhibition) and he won another gold medal, this time for *musen*, at the Third Domestic Exhibition in 1890. His main exhibit in 1890 was a pair of screens made of plaques of *musen* copies of paintings by famous Japanese painters mounted in wooden panels.

He executed several orders for the Imperial Household (including cloisonné models in the round) and in Meiji 28 (1896) was awarded the Medal of the Green Ribbon; in the citation for this award, he is credited not only with the invention of *musen*, but also with the invention of 360 new colours.

Watanabe Seitei (1851–1918) was a Japanese-style painter who specialised in realistic paintings of flowers and birds. He exhibited at the Paris Exposition of 1878, where he won a silver medal.

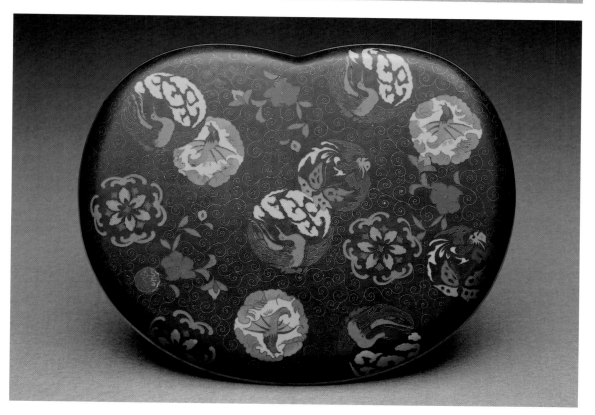

23
Vases
Sealed Namikawa Sosuke
Height 28 cm
Circa 1900

A pair of cloisonné enamel vases by Namikawa Sosuke, each of ovoid form decorated with flying and swimming mandarin ducks amid snow-laden reeds, worked in gold and silver wire and *musen* technique, on a pale grey ground, applied with *shakudo* mounts.

Sosuke rarely attempted or even wished to hide the wires totally; it was the ability to shade one colour into another that attracted him. This contrasts strongly with the practice of Namikawa Yasuyuki (no relation) who preferred perfectly monochrome backgrounds.

Interviewed by the New York Herald on 9 February 1896, when told that his work was attracting great attention in the United States, he was much pleased and remembered with gratitude the attention given his exhibit at the Columbian Exhibition (Chicago, 1893).

Sosuke had been told that his work had been criticised as too expensive; he answered '. . . it certainly is, when classed with the ordinary Cloisonné on the market; but I assure you that under my system, when the labor, time, repeated failures, &., incident to turning out a perfect gem are taken into consideration my valuations are not at all exhorbitant. Not a piece leaves my hands that does not represent many attempts and many failures and which is not the result of patient toil, wellnigh despairing . . . There is no certainty in what I essay. So much is left to accident in my burning process. The old methods were risky enough; mine are doubly doubtful'.

24
Vases
Stamped mark Hayashi Hachizaemon
Height 24.7 cm
Circa 1900

A pair of *musen* cloisonné enamel vases by Hayashi Hachizaemon decorated with purple, blue and white irises on a graduated pink to white ground.

With no wire visible, these vases bear a striking resemblance to the style of the contemporary porcelains of Makuzu Kozan (1842–1914) and of the Royal Copenhagen porcelain factory.

25
Vases
Signed Kawade within a double
gourd-shaped seal
Height 30.5 cm
Circa 1905

A pair of *moriage* (relief decorated) cloisonné enamel baluster-shaped vases by Kawade Shibataro each decorated with white lilies flowering from leafy stems on a graduated coffee-coloured ground, applied with silver mounts.

Kawade Shibataro was the chief worker at the Ando company. A versatile man, he is credited not only with the invention of *moriage* (somewhat doubtfully, see below) but also with the first successful Japanese *plique a jour* (see nos. 29, 30 and 31). The use of this low relief, *moriage* first appears about 1903; the Ando company exhibited some *moriage* vases at the St Louis Louisiana Purchase Exposition in 1904.

Ando Jubei whose company had perhaps opened in 1880 or 1881, was one of the first cloisonne makers to sell directly to foreigners, opening a shop in Ginza in 1887. By 1893 he was working for the Imperial Household Agency and he exhibited at the Columbian Exposition in Chicago in the same year.

26
Vase
Signed Kawade within the seal of
Ando
Height 36.5 cm
Circa 1905

A *moriage* cloisonné enamel vase by Kawade Shibataro, the shouldered body decorated with two pigeons in flight, one white, one in tones of dark green to mauve, on a graduated grey to pale green ground, worked with some silver wire and applied with silver mounts.

A characteristically high quality piece from the Ando company.

27
Vase
Signed Hattori sei
Height 35 cm
Circa 1905

An Imperial Presentation *moriage* cloisonné enamel vase by Hattori Tadasaburo decorated with a leafy stem of flowering yellow Hibiscus on a pale green ground, worked in silver wire; the neck with a white *kikumon* in gold wire.

Hattori Tadasaburo has, like Kawade, been credited with the first use of *moriage*. The Hattori company was one of five companies that received orders for cloisonne from the Imperial Household, the others being those of Namikawa Yasuyuki, Namikawa Sosuke, Ando Jubei and Hayashi Kodenji.

28
Vase
Signed Kinjiro sei
Height 25.5 cm
Circa 1900

A *tsuiki-jippo* enamel vase by Adachi Kinjiro decorated with a golden dragon writhing among waves on an ice-blue and purple ground, applied with silver mounts.

Adachi Kinjiro worked in Nagoya.
In this technique, transparent enamels are used over a silver body that has been worked in *repousse* and engraved, so that the apparent relief is mostly internal and does not raise the surface. In fact the dragon here is in slight relief, to emphasise the contrast with the background.

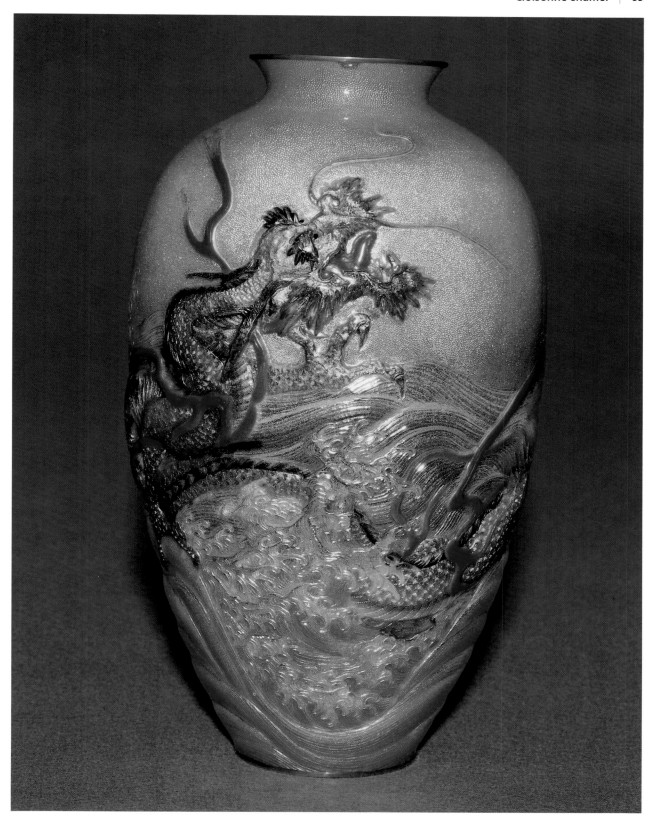

29
Vase
Signed Hattori
Height 23.5 cm
Circa 1910

A plique à jour *(shotai-jippo)* cloisonné enamel vase by Hattori Tadasaburo of waisted form decorated with autumnal leaves and berries on a pale green ground and with a central bulbous band of rippling waves in shades of blue, applied with silver mounts.

Ando Jubei is said to have brought back to Japan, from the World Fair in Paris of 1900, a piece of plique a jour enamel by Fernand Thesmar, from which Kawade Shibataro is said to have been able to imitate the technique. The Hattori company was one of the most consistently successful producers of pieces in this exceedingly difficult technique.

Plique a jour is made by the removal of the metal body after firing so that the enamel and the wires support themselves. The breakage rate was very high and consequently many pieces were originally sold with small cracks.

30
Bowl
Signed Hattori
Height 7 cm, diameter 12.7 cm
Circa 1910

A plique à jour cloisonné enamel bowl by Hattori Tadasaburo decorated with scattered chrysanthemum flowers in shades of purple, red and white on a deep crimson ground, applied with silver mounts.

31
Lamp
Unsigned
Height now 47 cm
Circa 1910

A plique à jour cloisonné enamel lamp, the shade of rounded hexagonal form decorated with numerous wild flowers and grasses in natural colours on a pale green ground. Now raised on a cloisonne enamel stand with butterflies and flowers on a pale blue ground.

Shibayama

The style of decorative inlay called Shibayama is usually easy to recognize and is easy to define, as long as it is understood that other families or workshops than that of the Shibayama family were producing wares in basically the same styles at the same time. There were plenty of competitors and imitators.

The style is based on the inlay of finely worked pieces of pearl-shell, ivory, coral, tortoise-shell, coconut-shell, horn and other materials that together make up a pattern, usually pictorial and in varying degrees of relief, into a ground of lacquer, ivory, wood or some other similar material. Most such pieces of good quality are modest in scale, varying from *tsuba* and *inro* to vessels (see no. 40) up through table screens (see nos. 37, 38 and 39) to quite large cabinets (see nos. 36 and 44). The very large pieces are nearly always relatively coarse and are probably not from the Shibayama workshop, though some may be fraudulently signed Shibayama.

The history of the family and of the workshop is very little known so only a family style is recognised as yet; we are unable to distinguish either the work of the successive generations of the family or of the various workmasters.

The style is generally said to be the invention of Onogi Senzo at Shibayama in Shimosa Province (today, Chiba Prefecture) during the An'ei period (1772–1781). Senzo is said to have moved to Edo (Tokyo) and changed his name to Shibayama Senzo. It is likely that this is too early a date, for at the First National Domestic Industrial Exposition in 1879, Shibayama Senzo and Shibayama Masayuki both won prizes for inlaid work; it would be more plausible to suggest that the style was more in tune with early Meiji taste and that Senzo's 'invention' of the style lay in the 1860s. One could, in fact, take the style back to that of Ritsuo (Ogawa Haritsu 1663–1747) though this would not mean very much. We exhibit here, as nos. 32 and 33, two pieces of lacquer which we see as forerunners of the Shibayama style, the first indicating a profusion of techniques in lacquer, the latter with some metal and pearl-shell inlay, not a rare combination at the time (late Edo), that could have been the point from which Senzo took his new style.

At the Second Domestic Industrial Exposition of 1881 and at the Third Domestic Industrial Exposition of 1890, Shibayama Soshichi and Shibayama Yasumasa both won prizes; at the latter, Soshichi's prize was for a panel of wood inlaid with a design of herons and lotus. It is tempting to draw comparisons with the panels of the cabinet exhibited here as no. 36, signed Yasunobu. Note the same first character to the name.

Comparisons between two of the table screens exhibited here, nos. 37 and 38, suggests that the somewhat crowded pictorial style of the larger panels of no. 37 was not only contemporary to, but also

made in the same workshop as the more open style panels of no. 38. In the latter sub-style the detail is lavished on the quality of the carving of the individual pieces of inlay, be they in ivory or anything else, rather than in the profusion of smaller pieces used to build up an intricate picture. It is the similarity of the smaller panels below the main panels that suggests that these are the products of one studio. Furthermore, this suggests that certain artists, presumably the best, made the larger panels that bore the main design of the screens, while other artists made the smaller panels and yet others presumably made the frame and other fittings. There was, then, a considerable degree of the division of labour in this high quality workshop, as one would expect.

This division of labour may go even further; there are known a number of cards on which are lightly glued Shibayama-style birds, insects etc. made of ivory, ready to be used as inlays. The individual pieces on these cards are of extremely fine quality, and ready-coloured; as they have not been exposed to light, these colours are remarkably fresh and bright. The backs of the pieces are flat; they must have been intended for flat surfaces such as table screens, *tsuba* or trays (no. 43), rather than for *inro* or for bottles (such as nos. 35 or 41) or jars (no. 40). The parts of the body such as the legs of birds or the antennae of insects that would not be rendered in ivory are indicated on the cards in ink. For the larger individual pieces, where there are only two or three pieces to the card (see illustration 2) a suggestion for their disposition is indicated in ink; for the small pieces, where there may be as many as twelve pieces on the card (see illustration 3), only the details are drawn in ink. It

2
Pair of painted ivory mandarin ducks
7.4 cm × 17 cm (card)

could be suggested that these were the products of outworkers who supplied the large workshops with images that could then be combined to form pictorial designs; this is a very different thing from the master making a drawing that would then be executed by the various workers involved in the factory production. The high quality of the individual pieces of carving on these cards precludes the possibility that only lesser workshops would stoop to such practices; it may very well have been general, at least at later dates, perhaps towards the end of the Meiji period. It must be admitted,

3
Twelve painted ivory birds
16.7 cm × 8 cm (card)

though, that we have no information on this point. It is tempting to suggest that the fine Shibayama-style *kodansu* in the Victoria and Albert Museum (W.23–1969) (Earle, 1986, no. 190) signed by Shinso and Shinsei and the Ozeki company, is decorated with cockerels from just such a source.

The body into which inlays were placed must have been made for the individual pieces at least in detail, for the lacquer, wood or ivory base had to be carved. It is likely, then, that the workshops employed their own lacquerers and ivory and wood carvers, though some things, such as the wood body of *inro* would have been bought in from specialists, just as lacquerers do today. Similarly, finished pieces could have been made to order for, or supplied to metalworkers to be used as panels in a metal body. We have chosen to include the filigree vase, no. 42 here under Shibayama rather than under metalwork for tenuous reasons of the balance of the catalogue rather than for reasons of its original production.

The Shibayama style is one that has suffered much from imitators, especially from those at the lower end of the scale of quality; the vast amount of very poor work has given a bad name to the work of the finest quality such as those pieces exhibited here. For that reason, perhaps, Shibayama wares have not received the attention that we believe to be their due; this may well be the first museum exhibition catalogue to do so.

32
Kashibako
Height 22 cm, width 17.2 cm,
length 41.8 cm
Late Edo period

A gold lacquer set of five trays and cover *(kashibako)* raised on a stand and enclosed in an overlapping pierced cover, elaborately decorated with trees, rocks and streams in a variety of lacquer techniques including *takamakie* (high relief), *hiramakie* (low relief), *kirigane* (inlay of pieces of cut gold foil) and *nashiji.*

The first half of the nineteenth century saw an elaboration of decoration in many materials; this was the foretaste of the Meiji period. In lacquer, the best quality pieces for the domestic connoisseurs' market used many techniques together on the same piece.

33
Box and cover
Height 8.2 cm, width 15.8 cm,
length 19.6 cm
Late Edo period

A lacquer box and cover with a fitted interior tray, the cover and sides with a pair of six-fold screens partly unfolded, on a *hirame* (large flakes of gold) ground. The screens decorated in *takamakie* and *hiramakie* with a woman, a sage playing a *koto,* Manchurian cranes, a cock and a hen and with 'the three friends' (pine, plum and bamboo) and with some inlay on a *kinji* ground, the screens outlined in *shakudo.* The interior tray with a trolley for books and scrolls, and a bunch of grasses on a *nashiji* ground.

The use of the *shakudo* borders to the screens, as well as the emphasised figures in dark lacquers suggest the origins of the Shibayama style. There is little pearl-shell inlay yet, but the balance of the figures in relation to the background, based originally, no doubt, on the work of Ritsuo, has changed into that that we shall see throughout the Meiji period.
The screens, with their Japanese subject matter, certainly suggest an Edo rather than an early Meiji date.

34
Kodansu
Height 23 cm, width 17.8 cm,
depth 23.3 cm
Early Meiji period

A *kodansu,* the exterior decorated with raised fans in gold lacquer *(kinji)* encrusted with various scenes of flowers and birds in pearl-shell, coral, ivory and other materials, and with silver fan sticks. The interior of the door with butterflies in polished lacquer *(togidashi)* on a so-called aventurine *(nashiji)* ground, and the drawers with stylised waterwheels under willow in *togidashi* on a black ground. Each fan signed in an ivory or pearl-shell plaque. With silver overhead handle and carved wood stand.

The shape, the *kodansu,* is a typical traditional shape, but the treatment of the decoration of the exterior, albeit again of traditional subjectmatter, marks this as a more international style piece, almost certainly made with a western client in mind. The interior is more conservative in taste; this seems typical, and the backs or interiors of many lacquer pieces seem more Japanese in taste than the exteriors.
The *kodansu* is not signed, but the fans are mostly signed with a seal mark; these signatures seem to mean little and are neither those of known lacquerers nor of painters. Among these seals are the names; Fukuyama, Furuyama, Yume, Hisamasa and Ranroku.
Kodansu of this size would have been used, if at all, for small items such as combs, hairpins and cosmetic items.

35
Bottles
Height 36.8 cm
Early Meiji period

A pair of double gourd bottles and stoppers decorated in typical style with panels of genre scenes including children playing and with smaller reserves of flowers on a false wood-grain *(mokume)* ground between formal petal-shaped borders and with a collar around the centre.

The double-gourd, *hyotan,* shape is found in every branch of Japanese applied arts and was much favoured in ceramics and lacquer for sake bottles such as these. In fact, these could not have been intended for use, for if filled with hot sake, they would have shed most of the inlay as the glues failed.
The relatively small size of the panels bearing inlaid scenes that have little to do with the overall decoration, and that are no more elaborate or vital to the decorative scheme than are the borders recalls the practice of extreme elaboration to be found in the contemporary ceramics of Kyoto.

36
Table cabinet
Signed on a pearl-shell plaque,
Shibayama Yasunobu and *kakihan*
Height 33.5 cm, width 33.2 cm
Early to middle Meiji period

An inlaid zelkova, coromandel and rosewood table cabinet, with two sliding doors enclosing a cupboard above two hinged doors enclosing five small drawers inlaid with birds and flowers and with flower arrangements and with fruits, shells and insects. The interior of the doors panelled with ivory.

The characters for Yasunobu can also be read Ekishin. Neither name seems to be adequately recorded.
This restrained style, where there is fine detail but also plenty of open background space is usually a mark of the better, possibly earlier pieces by members of the Shibayama family.

37
Table-screen
Signed (?) Ri
Height 20.3 cm
Middle Meiji period

A two-fold gold lacquer table-screen with two large panels minutely inlaid with a riverside scene of playful peasants amid flowering trees and bamboos in *togidashi, hiramakie* and *kirigane* on a *kinji* ground, above two smaller panels similarly decorated with still-life. The reverse similarly decorated but on a larger scale, with a pheasant and water-birds among flowering trees. The whole enclosed in an *oki-hirame* decorated frame.

The minutely detailed style of this screen sets it apart from the larger scale employed on nos. 38 and 39. There is no implication here that these three screens are from different workshops; on the contrary, the similarity of the lesser panels below the main panels suggests a common origin. The complexity of the picture, the small size of the individual pieces of inlay and the elaboration of the lacquer techniques used, do suggest an individual style within a workshop. Unfortunately the inadequacy both of the signatures and of the documentation of the Shibayama 'family' preclude further classification at this stage.
The Japanese tradition of humorous scenes, particularly of somewhat drunken peasants enjoying the cherry-blossom in spring, is well illustrated here.

38
Table-screen
Signed Masayoshi
Height 34.8 cm
Middle Meiji period

A two-fold table-screen inlaid with entertainers performing to a nobleman and a monk, in pearl-shell, hardstones and stained ivory on a gold lacquer ground, above panels with bouquets of flowers and fans. The reverse with *togidashi* panels of cranes and irises, above panels of pinks, all within an ivory frame.

Compare the scale of the figures and the degree of carving of the individual pieces of inlay in whatever medium with that of no. 37. Attention is focussed on the scene depicted and not diffused by a multiplicity of small details, while there is almost no variation of the plain gold lacquer background. The reverse is as finely wrought as the front, albeit in the different material.

39
Table-screen
Signed Masataka (or Masaoka)
Height 20.8 cm
Middle Meiji period

A two-fold table-screen inlaid with a group of cockerels and chickens under a flowering prunus tree, in carved ivory and coloured pearl-shell, hardstones and coconutshell, on a gold lacquer ground, above panels of flowers. The reverse with exotic carp swimming beneath a wistaria in restrained *hiramakie* and *togidashi,* above panels of flying phoenix.

The reverse scene is very finely detailed in conservative taste in lacquer, to a degree that would have made it fully acceptable as the face of a screen had contemporary tastes been more austere.

40
Jar and cover
Signed on the base on a red lacquer
plaque Yasutada
Raised on an ivory stand
Height 18.5 cm
Middle to late Meiji period

A lobed jar and cover decorated with four panels, outlined in silver and inlaid with scenes of flowers and birds on a *kinji* ground. The domed cover and the background with elaborate overlapping panels in coloured lacquers and gold, mostly in *hiramakie*, of patterns, stylised birds and flowers and butterflies. The cover with an enamelled silver lotus flower.

The characters for the name could also be read Ekinao.
As with no. 35 the panels of inlaid scenes are no more important to the decorative scheme than are the elaborate geometrical patterns of the borders and of the lid. The whole is highly remeniscent of contemporary Kyoto earthenware in Satsuma style.

41
Vase
Signed on a pearl-shell plaque
Baigetsu
Height 31.7 cm
Late Meiji period

A tall gold lacquer vase with slightly flaring lotus-petalled neck and quadrelobed bulbous body decorated with two reserves of silver-edged panels encrusted with figures under a flowering cherry tree and with a woman feeding carp from a sake cup. The body decorated with *oki-hirame* (relatively large squares of gold foil laid in an overall regular pattern), and with *hiramakie* mon and a *togidashi* floral band and butterflies. Raised on a tall lobed base and with a silver dragon clutching a crystal ball (the 'sacred jewel') twined around the neck.

As in nos. 35 and 40 the background elaboration of lacquer techniques are as important as the inlaid panels. The panels themselves have the complexity of those of the screen (37) above but are overshadowed by the large-scale dragon coiled around the flared neck of the vessel. The bracketted foot, a common shape in later Meiji works in all media, derives from the wood, ivory or lacquer stand on which earlier pieces were placed, but which has now become integral (see also, e.g. no. 12).

42
Vase
Signed Tomomitsu
Height 33.5 cm
Late Meiji period

A tall hexagonal vase with flattened shoulders and a trumpet neck, the body in filigree silver inset with *kinji* gold lacquer panels inlaid with flowers, trees and birds in pearl-shell, ivory, tortoiseshell and coconutshell. The shoulders also in filigree silver and with six modelled ho-o birds. The neck and bracketted foot with formal patterns of flowers in cloisonné enamel.

It is difficult to know to which part of this vessel the signature refers. Was it made by a Shibayama lacquerer and mounted in this elaborate filigree and cloisonné casing, or was it the work of a metal artist who added some Shibayama panels? As the panels are not of the finest quality, while the metalwork is so fine, it might be suggested that this piece could be classified as metalwork; it is here included in the lacquer section as it does not relate closely to any included metalwork. To some extent, this could be seen as a summation of late Meiji taste.

43
Tray
Signed on a pearl-shell plaque
Shibayama
Height 42.5 × 61 cm
Late Meiji period

A rectangular lacquer tray with inverted corners and curved edge, with a central concave-sided panel of *kinji* lacquer inlaid with a complex scene of the seven sages of the bamboo grove; their robes, some bamboo leaves and other details richly inlaid. The border with stylised gold *ho-o* birds and *kiri-mon* (Paulownia-leaf crests), and the outer border in wood-grain *(mokume)*.

Clearly an exhibition piece, this work, signed solely Shibayama may be the work of the master, needing no qualificatory given name. The open appearance of the scene belies the intricacy of the inlay in this most conservative of subjects, the very choice of subject suggesting a Japanese rather than an international exhibition.

44
Cabinet
Height 24.6 cm
Late Meiji period

A silver-mounted miniature cabinet with silver-framed cupboard doors and similar drawers arranged in break-front form, each inset with an ivory panel inlaid with trees, birds, flowers and bouquets in pearl-shell and ivory, above and below a central open section with a symmetrical arrangement of drawers and shelves decorated with flowers, in gold lacquer. The main silver body decorated with *manji* diaper, flowers and a view of Mount Fuji.

The use of ivory as the base in which to inlay with other materials is a forerunner of innumerable later essays in the Shibayama style, mostly for export, and including anything from vast canopied elephant figures and tusk vases to buttons and bridge-markers. This exhuberant cabinet, almost too showy for its own good, is another summation of late Meiji taste; quite specifically for the export market, the quality is nevertheless fine but it seems that each element of the decoration is in competition with the others rather than forming a cohesive scheme.

Appendix

The technique of cloisonné enamel
Rosemary Zeeman

Cloisonné enamelling, or enamelling into little cells, is, at its simplest, a matter of forming thin, ribbon shaped wires into a pattern, laying these narrow side uppermost onto a metal base and filling the enclosures made by the pattern with finely ground glass of differing colours. The whole is then put into a very hot furnace for a very short time. As the metal becomes hot, so too does the ground glass, which melts and forms little lakes of colour confined by the cloisonné wires. Provided a sufficiently high temperature is reached, the glass bonds itself to the metal base and wires, and when cool, the area can be made level and polished, with the tops of the wires showing as a delicate pattern dividing the colours one from another.

The above account, while essentially correct, is nevertheless a gross simplification of what actually happens when a piece of cloisonné work is in progress. At each stage there are alternatives to be considered, choices made, dangers avoided and mistakes rectified.

The metals most commonly used for enamelling are gold, silver and copper, and, for best results with regard to colour, each of these metals should be as pure as possible. The colours in enamels are the result of the addition of metal oxides to a basic clear enamel (or flux), and these oxides may react with the metal of the base plate. If this plate is itself an alloy, it is a mixture of several metals, each of which may react differently with the enamel, and the risk of the colour changing or clouding when fired is greater than if the metal is pure. Compromises do have to be made, however, in cases where the pure metal would not be sturdy enough, fine silver, for example, is very soft and bends easily, so that any enamel on its surface risks being cracked unless the fine silver is strengthened by being set or supported by a stronger frame. Similarly, fine gold is very soft and so is unsuitable for many pieces of work, even though some colours, particularly the reds (derived from gold oxide) show at their most brilliant over fine gold.

Having chosen a metal, then, the enameller will begin work. On the bench will be a metal sheet, or bowl, or vase, and a length of cloisonné wire. This wire will be very thin, possibly 0.1mm or 0.2mm, and about 1mm wide. On a piece of paper will be drawn out the pattern which is to appear on the finished piece. Using fingers and tweezers or very fine pliers, and using the drawing as a guide, short pieces of wire are bent in the shapes required, until the whole pattern has been translated into wires. A second copy of the paper pattern, with double sided tape over it, is a help here, so that wires as they are shaped can be positioned on the drawing, progress monitored and distortions prevented. As the wire is ribbon shaped, and standing on its narrow edge, straight pieces are rarely used as they do not stand up easily, and would almost certainly fall over as the enamel melts in the kiln. This is one reason why most cloisonné patterns are all in terms of curved wires; even where the wires appear straight, in geometric patterns, it is usually a careful arrangement of bent wires so disposed to give the appearance of a construction of straight ones. Only with wires which are round or square in cross-section can one feel secure in using a straight piece, and such wires bring other difficulties with them: a wire of sufficient diameter to give enough height to contain the required depth of enamel will, when ground down and polished, be much wider than the ribbon wire whose width is constant, and the pattern will lose in delicacy as a result. Similarly, square wires, to be of sufficient height, will also be too thick.

Before transferring the wires to the base plate it is essential to rid that plate of all oxides and grease, otherwise the glass will not bond properly to the metal and any type of dust will show as black specks or cloudy areas in the fired enamel. The cleaning is done by heating and then 'pickling' in a dilute solution of sulphuric acid. This removes the oxides, and the metal is then rinsed under running water while being scrubbed with a glass brush and the odd spot of saliva to neutralise any trace remaining of the acid. When the water runs smoothly over the surface of the metal, it is clean, and from then onwards must be handled only by the edges. It is more or less impossible to clean the wires in the same way without distorting them, and as the wires are usually fine silver or fine gold they will not have oxidised to any great extent. Copper is another matter – the wire will have been cleaned before being bent, but does present a problem at each firing because of the thick layer of oxides (known as fire scale) which forms on uncovered areas in the kiln and on cooling flies off as black flakes and thereby presents a great hazard for the next firing unless removed. Once the wires are securely fastened to the base they can be gently brushed with a glass brush to remove this scale.

How then to secure the wires to the base plate is the next problem. If they move about while being filled with the first layer of enamel the colours will mix and become uncontrollable. In order to avoid movement the wires may be soldered to the base or stuck to it in one of two ways. Soldering is not usually chosen, as enamel may change colour or chip away where it comes into contact with solder (which is an alloy). Only where a piece is on a relatively large scale and has to be very sturdy will the wires be soldered to the base. Generally they are stuck in position with a glue; the ancients used glue made from fish scales, gum tragacanth has been used for centuries, and today there are other products available. They all share the essential property of burning away leaving no trace behind them. If the first layer of enamel is to be an overall layer of flux, as is often the case when copper is used, the wires can be placed on this layer, and when fired will sink down into the melting flux and be held firmly when cool. As the piece is withdrawn from the kiln, still rosy with heat, there are a few seconds, before the enamel hardens, during which wires can be reshaped with tweezers and pressed down with spatulas to make sure of a good adhesion at the base and good joints and curves within the pattern – clearly there is time for only a few corrections and ideally there will be none to make. When flux is not being used as a base layer, and colours are being laid directly onto the metal, the wires may be stuck down with the glue mentioned. After the first firing they will be secure. Some experienced enamellers can lay the first layer of colour without sticking down the wires at all; this takes skill and nerve, and success depends to some extent on the nature of the pattern.

The wires secure, the colours must be prepared. Enamels may be either opaque or transparent; if the latter the underlying metal base shows through and will affect the look of the finished piece. Today, they can be bought in lump form or ready ground to the texture of sand. Lump form is preferable as it has a longer shelf life and is reputed to give a more brilliant colour if ground just prior to being used. The grinding is done in a mortar, preferably made from agate which is very hard. The lump is covered with water and gently tapped with the pestle to break it into smaller pieces. The water is then drained off and grinding proper begins, until the enamel chips are grains of the desired size – usually about that of fine sand. If the piece of work on hand requires it, the grains will be sifted through meshes after being washed. Water is poured onto the enamel in the mortar, and given a quick stir with the pestle. For the first three or four washes the water will become cloudy, and after a wait of a few seconds must be thrown off leaving behind the bulk of the enamel, and taking with it specks of dust, oxides from the surface of the enamel lump, and some of the finer grains. After five or six washings the water will be clear and the enamel have a bright and sparkling look to it. Two more washes in purified water and it is ready for use. There will be several colours to prepare in this way, and they should be stored under purified water in a shallow non-metallic container, and covered. If kept air tight, they can be stored this way for several days, but for best results it is better to use them as soon as possible after grinding.

When the time arrives for the laying in of the colours, they are drained of most of the covering water and the containers tilted slightly, so that the enamel is presented as barely damp in the highest part of the dish and increasingly waterlogged down towards the lowest. The placement of the enamel is controlled to a large extent by the water around it; it is therefore very important that it should be damp enough to be moved over the surface in a controlled way, but not so wet that the water swills over the surface taking the grains with it into the wrong place. The enameller will, therefore, choose quite carefully which degree of dampness to pick up, and will keep a sharp eye on the areas already filled. If these become dry before the whole surface is covered, water will be fed into them to keep them under control. The traditional tool in the West for picking up the enamel and laying it in position is a sharpened goose quill. Fine sable brushes are also used. Very small amounts are picked up by the point and deposited side by side like tiny molehills in the area being worked. The side of the point can then be used to even out these small deposits until the area is covered by a very thin, even layer of grains. The piece will then be tapped gently along one edge which helps to settle down the grains more closely and evenly, and thus forcing to the surface not only the water but also the air which is, inevitably, trapped between them. Tiny though these air pockets are, they will, during the firing, expand and form bubbles if they cannot escape to the surface. Sometimes this process of compaction is helped by pressing down on the surface of the enamel with small spatulas or even wads of clean cotton cloth shaped into cushion-like pads. Correctly handled, these pads will compact the grains and draw off the water at the same time without disturbing the placement of the colours. Any trace of moisture will, during the firing, turn into steam, burst through the enamel possibly throwing it out of place, and causing bubbles and pits in the surface. For this reason it is important that the piece should be thoroughly dry before being fired, and this is usually achieved by standing it on top of the kiln for a few minutes, or by holding it in front of the open mouth of the kiln and rotating it. At this stage the most careful handling is essential. Any sudden movement during the transference of the piece from its drying position into the kiln will almost certainly shake off sections of the dry enamel, and the enameller will have to return to the point of laying in fresh.

A good enameller will always try to proceed by very thin layers, each one fired and the next added, so that a piece may be fired 6–10 times before the enameller judges that the cloisons are well enough filled for the levelling and polishing process to begin. Not all pieces require so many firings, but some do. The advantages of proceeding in this way are several: it reduces the chances of cracking and flaking of the enamel during the cooling period, improves the clarity of transparent enamels by reducing the number of bubbles trapped within each layer, and permits the laying of several colours, one over another, which can produce subtler colours and beautiful effects. At some stage in this process this gold or silver foil, (always pure) may be laid onto the enamel, pricked with a sharp point to allow air underneath to escape, and fired down onto the surface. Subsequent layers will then be particularly brilliant where they lie over the foil.

While drying, the work will rest on a stand made either of ceramic or iron or stainless steel or titanium. One looks for a stand which will not weaken in the heat of the kiln nor form dust producing oxides. Titanium is very good in both these respects, and has the advantage over ceramic in that it can be had in the form of mesh which can be cut and bent into whatever shape forms the best support. Where work is enamelled on both sides, or in the round, the design of the support is most important as it must provide a stable base for the piece while touching at as few points as possible, in order not to mark the enamel or become stuck to it. When completely dry the piece is lifted, on its stand, by long-handled tongs or forks and placed well into the kiln which will be at a temperature of about 800°C–900°C, bright orange in colour and will be either electric or gas fired. Today, most enamellers work with small kilns which often have spy holes in the door. If not, the door can be opened a fraction at intervals to check the progress of the enamel. Under the influence of the heat the enamel first turns black and the grains seem to bunch together slightly before beginning to melt and flow, first into a rippled surface and finally into a glassy-smooth one, at which point the work must be swiftly withdrawn. The time in the kiln will be between 30 seconds and two or three minutes depending on the size of the piece, the heat of the kiln and the colours being fired. Some colours require more heat to flow: these are known at the 'hard' colours as opposed to the 'soft' ones requiring less heat. The reds, particularly those leaning towards orange, are difficult in that they melt at temperatures well below those of most other colours and easily burn black if left in the kiln beyond their melting time. Nor do they tolerate many firings, so that work including these reds has to be organised with these restrictions in mind.

Once the piece is withdrawn from the kiln it is put to one side to cool down very slowly so that the strains resulting from the different rates of expansion and contraction of metal and glass are kept to a minimum. As it is cooling the colours reappear, and it can therefore be a very exciting or disappointing moment. Sudden changes in temperature at this stage result in cracks in the enamel. In order to avoid this, work, especially where the enamel is as thick as the metal base, will be counter-enamelled (i.e. on the back) and this does much to reduce the risk of cracking. Once the piece is cold it is cleaned and examined for specks and bubbles which can be ground out with a diamond-tipped drill, or carborundum stone and the grindings washed away. A fresh layer of enamel is then laid, paying special attention to the filling of the holes, dried and refired. Work continues in this way until the fired enamel is at the top of the cloisonné wires. The piece is then ground smooth with carborundum stones or diamond-impregnated papers, under running water, until the whole surface is level and matt, with no shiny areas of enamel or 'dips' showing. If a polished surface is required, as it usually is, the piece may be refired briefly, which will restore the highly reflective, glassy surface, or it may be hard polished with increasingly fine carborundum or diamond papers, or with fine pumice powder used wet on a felt mop on a polishing machine. This slower method of finishing produces a perfectly smooth and lustrous surface which is regarded by many enamellers as the most desirable. The polishing will level and brighten both enamel and metal, and the piece is finished as far as the enamelling goes.

Vases and bowls have vulnerable edges at the foot and lip, and these are usually protected by metal edging either applied after the enamelling, or by the retaining walls present before the enamelling process began. Being glass, enamel is always vulnerable to sudden blows, and the edges are particularly vulnerable, It is therefore important to work out beforehand exactly how those edges will be protected in the finished piece.

Bibliography

Japanese sources

Nakagawa Chisaki (ed.) 'Meiji no kogei' *Nihon no bijutsu* 41, (1969).

Katori Masahiko, *Chukin kindaisiko*, (Chukinka Kyokai, Tokyo, 1957).

Tani Shinichi and Noma Shinroku, *Nihon bijutsu jiten* (Toyoda Shuppan, 1952, 38th edition, 1990).

Wakayama Takeshi, *Toso kinko jiten*, (Yuzankaku, Tokyo, 1984).

Yoshida Mitsukuni, *Kyo shippo monyo shu*, (Tankosha, Tokyo, 1986)

English language sources

Baekland, Frederick (ed.) *Imperial Japan; the art of the Meiji era, 1868–1912,* (New York, 1980).

Bowes, J.L., *Japanese enamels,* (Liverpool, 1884).

Bowes, J.L., *Notes on shippo,* (London, 1895).

Brinkley, Capt. F., *Japan; its history, arts and literature, VII, Pictorial and applied art,* (London, 1904).

Bruschke-Johnson, Lee, 'Japanese cloisonné in the Walters Art Gallery', *The Journal of The Walters Art Gallery,* 47, 1989, pp. 3–12.

Coben, L.A. and Ferster, D.C., *Japanese cloisonné,* (New York and Tokyo, 1982).

A dictionary of Japanese art terms, (Tokyo Bijutsu, Tokyo, 1990).

Earle, Joe (ed.) *Japanese art and design; the Toshiba Gallery* (London 1986).

Fairley, Malcolm, *Japanese enamels of the Golden Age,* (Barry Davies Oriental Art, London, 1990).

Fairley, Malcolm, *Masterpieces of Meiji metalwork,* (Barry Davies Oriental Art, London, 1991).

Gabbert Avitabile, Gunhild, *Die Ware aus dem Teufelsland; Chinesisch und Japanische cloisonné- und champleve-Arbeiten von 1400 bis 1900,* (Frankfurt am Main, 1981).

Harada Jiro, 'Japanese art and artists of today', IV, Wood and ivory carving, *The Studio,* 51, 1910. pp. 103–119.

Harada Jiro, 'Japanese art and artists of today', V, Metalwork, *The Studio,* 52, 1911, pp. 95–105.

Harada Jiro, 'Japanese art and artists of today', VI, Cloisonné enamel-work. *The Studio,* 53, 1911, pp. 271–286.

Jahss, Melvin and Betty, *Inro and other miniature forms of Japanese lacquer art,* (London, 1970).

Ponting, Herbert G., *In Lotus-land Japan,* (London, 1910).

Robinson, B.W., *The Baur Collection, Geneva, Japanese sword-fittings and associated metalwork,* (Geneva, 1980).

Schaap, Robert (ed.), *Meiji; Japanese art in transition,* (The Hague, 1987).

Glossary

Bugaku	A traditional dance-drama of refined, aristocratic type
Busshi	Carver of Buddhistic images (in this context)
fuchi	Ring around a sword-hilt, next to the guard (en suite with the *kashira* q.v.)
go	Art name
hiramakie	Flat lacquer decoration (i.e. no relief)
hirame	Metallic particles in graded sizes used in lacquer decoration
hoho	Phoenix
honzogan	Flat inlay into metal
hyotan	Gourd
inro	Small compartmented medicine box suspended below the sash
iroe-honzogan	Coloured flat inlay
iroe-takazogan	Coloured raised inlay
kago	Two-wheeled carriage
kakihan	Artist's written seal or 'logo'
kashibako	Compartmented sweetmeat box
kashira	Cap on the end of a sword hilt (en suite with *fuchi* q.v.)
katana	Long sword
kikumon	The sixteen-petalled chrysanthemum badge of the Imperial Family
kinji	Gold lacquer background
kinkoku	Honorific word attached to signature (i.e. 'respectfully', etc.)
kirigane	Metallic foil cut to various sizes, used in lacquer decoration
kodansu	Small chest of drawers
koro	Incense burner
koto	Japanese ten-stringed 'harp'
kozuka	Small knife accompanying a short sword
manji	Swastika-like pattern
menuki	Decorated rivet-cover on a sword-hilt
mokume	Wood-grain decorative effect
moriage	Low relief on cloisonné (in this context)
musen	Wire-less cloisonné
nashiji	'Aventurine' effect in lacquer; fine gold dust
oki-hirame	Large squares of cut metal foil used in lacquer decoration
okimono	Model or free-standing figure
oni	Small demon
plique à jour	Cloisonné enamel from which the supporting body has been removed
repousse	Relief worked from the reverse
rui	Formal pattern based on a fungus
sentoku	Brass
shakudo	Dark pickled metal alloy
shibuichi	Silvery pickled metal alloy
shippo	Cloisonné enamel
shotai-jippo	plique à jour enamel (q.v.)
takazogan	Raised inlay on metal
togidashi	Lacquer technique in which the design is made visible by repeated coating and polishing
tsuba	Sword guard
tsuiki-jippo	Transparent enamel

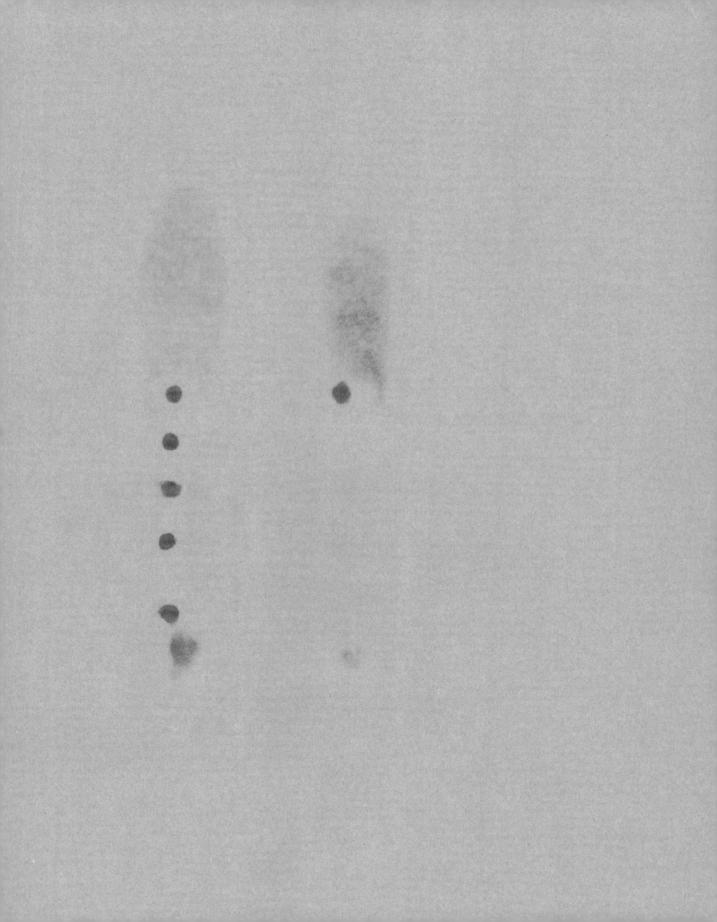

10/09